1 MONTH OF
FREE
READING

at

www.ForgottenBooks.com

By purchasing this book you are eligible for one month membership to ForgottenBooks.com, giving you unlimited access to our entire collection of over 1,000,000 titles via our web site and mobile apps.

To claim your free month visit:

www.forgottenbooks.com/free295924

ISBN 978-0-656-02860-3
PIBN 10295924

For support please visit www.forgottenbooks.com

REPORT

AT THE

ANNUAL MEETING

OF

he Handel and Haydn Society,

MAY 27, 1867,

BY THE PRESIDENT.

REPORT

TO THE MEMBERS OF

The Handel and Haydn Society,

AT THEIR

FIFTY-SECOND ANNUAL MEETING,

HELD IN BUMSTEAD HALL, MAY 27, 1867.

BY

J. BAXTER UPHAM, M.D.

PRESIDENT OF THE SOCIETY.

PRINTED AT THE REQUEST OF THE MEMBERS.

BOSTON:

ROCKWELL & ROLLINS, PRINTERS,

122 WASHINGTON STREET.

1867.

REPORT.

Gentlemen, Members of the Handel and Haydn
Society : —

By the recent revision of the By-laws, it is
now made the duty of the President of this society to present, at its annual meeting, a written
report, giving an abstract of the doings of the
society for the year, and offering any sugges-
tions and recommendations which the occasion
may seem to demand. In compliance with the
letter and spirit of this requirement, I beg leave
to submit the following : —

There have been nine regular meetings of the
Government during the year, to attend to business, and to consult in various ways for the inter-
ests of the corporation. The society has been
five times called together for the admission of
members and the transaction of other business.
At all these meetings a gratifying degree of una-
nimity and good feeling has prevailed. Thirty-

one gentlemen have been admitted to membership during the year, eight have been discharged, and four have resigned.

The rehearsals — thirty-two in number — were commenced in Bumstead Hall on the 30th day of September, and have continued weekly, without interruption, and with the addition of the usual extra meetings for practice prior to a public performance, until Easter. These rehearsals have been, on the whole, more punctually and more fully attended than at any previous season within my recollection, — a certain and sure augury of good for the future.

Six public performances in the Music Hall have taken place, of which the following was the programme for the season, viz.: —

Nov. 25. — Mendelssohn's St. Paul.
Dec. 23. — Handel's Messiah.
Feb. 17. — Handel's Jephtha.
Feb. 24. — Haydn's Creation.
April 20. — { Rossini's Stabat Mater, and
{ Mendelssohn's Hymn of Praise.
April 21. — Mendelssohn's Elijah.

These great works have been presented after much and careful preparation, with a liberal expenditure of means, under an experienced and

accomplished conductor, in a manner worthy of
the highest praise, and which I do not hesitate
to say would reflect honor upon any city in the
world. They have been participated in by a
chorus numbering now nearly five hundred efficient voices, an orchestra of fifty instruments,
and with the accompaniment of an organ in the
very first rank of excellence, under a master's
hand. Among the solo artists, in addition to
those resident with us, and whom we at all times
honor and respect, a Parepa and a Phillips have
delighted to lend their aid. The audiences have
been commensurate with the occasions ; they
have been drawn, not alone from our own appreciative community, but largely also from distant
towns and cities ; and I am happy to add, as
you have learned from your Treasurer's report,
that, for once, the season has resulted in a satis-
factory pecuniary success.

In the list of oratorios above given, it will be
seen that an addition has been made to our yet
too limited *repertoire.* The Jephtha of Handel
was performed by us, in the season now just
passed, for the first time. It is to be hoped that
in future our musical horizon will be extended,
till all of the acknowledged master-works of

Handel at least shall be comprised within its scope ; and I think the time is not far distant when we may venture beyond, upon some of the great choral achievements of Sebastian Bach.

The library, as appears by the report of our excellent Librarian, is in good condition, and, notwithstanding some mysterious losses, which are greatly to be deplored, is still in the way of growth and improvement. From the detailed statements of Mr. Chickering, made last year, I quote the following; as giving in brief the character and extent of the library at that time : —

"During the season, in accordance with a vote of the government, a new catalogue has been prepared, and the whole library rearranged by the Assistant Librarian, Mr. Bedlington. The present excellent arrangement of the books, and the completeness of the new catalogue, show how faithfully this duty has been performed. In the library-room, each shelf, case, or compartment is numbered or lettered, and the books or music contained in each indicated on the catalogue ; this shows how many we have of each edition or form of a work, the number of parts for each voice, and the number of parts for each orchestral instrument. The complete orchestral music for each work is now kept in its particular portfolio, which is lettered, marked, or numbered to correspond with the catalogue. In order to give the society an idea of the present condition of the library, I have prepared the following sta-tistics : —

" Of the works owned by us there is an aggregate of 9,673 separate vocal parts. Of these, 6,210 are single-voice parts, and 3,463 are in vocal score for chorus. The orchestral music consists of 1,174 separate instrumental parts. Of orchestral or piano-forte scores, we possess 124 volumes. In addition, we have 270 volumes of various works not in actual use at the present day, but many of them possessing rare interest to our older members.

" The following is a list of works of which we own sufficient vocal music for five hundred voices, and an orchestra of sixty instruments: The Creation, Elijah, Eli, Festival Overture, Hymn of Praise, Israel in Egypt, Forty-second Psalm, Judas Maccabæus, Messiah, and St. Paul. A small addition of vocal and instrumental music to the following works would suffice for the present number of the society : Destingen Te

Deum, Jephtha, Joseph, Mozart's Requiem, Ode to St. Cecilia, and Samson.

"Of the following works, although of many we own a large number of copies, we should require large additions of vocal and instrumental parts to enable us to perform them with the present number of the society: Alexander's Feast, David, Hymn of the Night, Joshua, Last Judgment, The Martyrs, Moses in Egypt, Mount of Olives, Mount Sinai, The Seasons, Seven Sleepers, Transient and Eternal, Stabat Mater, and Solomon.

"From the foregoing, it appears that very valuable additions have been made to our library during the past season, and that great improvements have been made in its arrangement and means of care and preservation. Now, more than ever, I feel it is entitled to be considered the most valuable library of sacred music in the country."

To the above enumeration must be added seventy copies of Rossini's Stabat Mater; and one hundred and sixty copies of Jephtha, in vocal score, octavo edition, with such instrumental parts as were required by the enlarged orchestra now employed,—the increase of the library during the past year.

It may be proper to speak, in this connection, of a proposition which has more than once been mooted in the meetings of the government, and which I earnestly hope may soon be carried into effect. It is the preparation of the annals of the society for publication. Such a history would, I doubt not, be a most acceptable possession to all the present and past members of our venerable association, and would not be without interest to others who have at heart the welfare of the cause we are endeavoring to support and to advance. The time for such a work, if it is ever to be accomplished, ought not to be much longer delayed. Our earliest associates are rapidly passing away. All the original members are now dead. In a brief while, it will be impossible to find among the living any in whose memory lingers a picture of the early trials and struggles through which our now sturdy and vigorous manhood has been attained. I would recommend this subject, therefore, to the serious consideration of the future board.

Suffer from me now a few words of comment, bearing upon the present condition and future prospects of the society. It has been my custom in these reports both to praise and commend where commendation was just, and freely to point out any faults and defects that seemed to exist, with a view, if possible, to suggest their remedy. Such criticisms and comments have always been received in the same spirit of kindness and good-will with which they have been offered.

One of the crying evils upon which I have many times animadverted, is that of *absenteeism at rehearsals*. In this, as I have said, I have observed the past season a manifest change for the better. Still the fault exists, and is now as ever (I say it unhesitatingly) the chief obstacle in the way of our rapid advance towards a more perfect interpretation of the great works we have, for so many years, been endeavoring to understand and to appreciate.

I am aware of the difficulties which, in an association like ours, stand in the way of an absolute attendance, on the part of every member, upon the meetings required, during the seven or eight months of the year, for practice and rehearsal, nor are such delinquencies confined, by any means, to our own body. They are recognized and felt in every association of the kind where the members voluntarily band themselves together for a kindred object. And, as a consequence, the most rigid rules have often been adopted, to anticipate and to obviate, if possible, the difficulty. The London Sacred Harmonic Society, for this reason, found it expedient to have printed and sent to every member a circular, from which I quote the following : —

"It is quite obvious" (say the Committee) "that the efficiency of the public performances "must, in a great degree, depend upon the atten- "tion previously bestowed at the rehearsals; and "that the reputation of the society and its claims "for public support are liable to be materially "affected by the neglect of those means which "rehearsals alone afford, for acquiring a thorough "knowledge of the music which is there practised, "and a facility in executing it with becoming ac- "curacy and expression. However much reason "there may be for congratulation upon the gen- "eral character of the society's performances, and "for considering them as at least equal to any "others of the same kind in this country, it cannot "be denied that there is still room for further im- "provement, and that occasions do happen in

" which many of the peculiar features of a compo-
" sition are not properly developed, through want
" of that *regular* and *combined* attention at rehear-
" sals, which is absolutely essential to a correct
" and effective performance. The Committee feel
" it their imperative duty, not only to urge the
" importance of this subject upon the notice of the
" members and assistants, but to endeavor, also, to
" ckech the inconveniences which have resulted
" from a neglect of it." And the Committee, in
commenting upon this appeal, say further, that
"inasmuch as punctual attendance at rehearsals
" can alone secure efficiency of performance, they
" feel that they would not be acting up to their
" duty to the society, if they should hesitate to dis-
" pense with the assistance of any members who
" did not comply with such reasonable and essen-
"tial requirements." And they subsequently went
so far as to require their candidates for admission to pledge themselves beforehand to the con-
scientious observance of these obligations ; this
in a society similarly constituted with our own,
but by some twenty years our junior, — a society,
too, whose meetings for practice were, at that
time, held on some evening in every week
throughout the year.

I have hitherto felt an embarrassment in urging this subject upon the attention of members at our meetings, arising from the fact that thôse who most needed such admonition were the ones most likely to be then absent; and the same remark will apply at the present time. It might be well, therefore, if we were to imitate the example of our London associate in this respect, and send a similar appeal to every individual member of our society. Did we but *insist* with equal pertinacity upon such constant and punctual attendance at our evenings for practice, who knows to what a summit of excellence it might be possible for us to attain?

I have heretofore alluded to the disposition manifested on the part of some members to leave their places in the choir, at a public performance, before the end of the oratorio ; and I am glad to be able to record a marked improvement in this respect, for the season just closed. I wish I could say as much for those on whom has devolved the duty of rendering the more prominent roles in our oratorios. Such indecorous haste in leaving the platform, as is sometimes seen on their part, ill comports with the dignity and sincerity of a true artist. Aside from the bad example it sets to the house, it cannot be looked upon with indifference by either the orchestra or chorus. It is to be hoped that, hereafter, in their engagements with artists of whatever standing or renown, the government will stipulate for their *presence*, at all events, till the close of the performance. Let me heartily commend you for better remembering your part of this duty. Be assured it is known and recognized by that appreciative few in every audience who would not willingly have the closing periods, which a great composer has patiently added to his immortal work, shorn of a single ray of their glory.

One or two more points, of minor consideration, perhaps, but which are yet, in my estimation, of sufficient importance to be mentioned here, and I have done with this part of my subjcet.

The number of our active and associate members — of those, I mean, who occasionally, at least, participate in the rehearsals and public performauces of the society at the present time — is not far from six hundred. Counting, in addition, the names which are enrolled upon the Secretary's list, but who rarely appear at any of our meetings, the aggregate far exceeds this number.

In such large masses, unless the utmost order and system is observed, there must needs be some hurrying and crowding in the formation of the choir at a public performance. Some instances of discomfort have arisen from this source, during the past season, which have come to my notice. It was, in part, to obviate diffi- culties of this nature, that, a few years since, the staff of Superintendents, so called, was organ- ized, having charge of the several departments of the chorus. As our numbers increase, the duties of these gentlemen become more impor- tant and more arduous. It becomes a question, even now, whether it will not further subserve the comfort and convenience of every member of the chorus, if the plan of numbering the seats of the choir, in both the upper and lower halls, be adopted, so that each member shall henceforth occupy, at all times, at rehearsals and in public performances, his own appropriate place. This is the plan pursued in London, and elsewhere, in associations of similar extent with our own, and serves the double purpose of a more just and orderly disposition of the members in taking their seats, and in some sort registering their presence or absence whenever required.

And while upon the subject of the duties of superintendents, I would again suggest that they acquaint themselves with the name of every one belonging to the department under their especial charge, so as to be able to report the attendance or non-attendance of every member at the meetings of the society. A very little exercise of observation and memory will enable them to do this without difficulty.

I would call the attention of the examining committee to the fact that, in order to the proper balancing of the chorus, there is still room for a considerable increase among the tenors; while, at the same time, the other parts might be rendered more efficient by the judicious addition of a limited number of really good and telling voices.

I cannot forbear a word of commendation, in this place, upon the liberal policy adopted by the government, during the past season, in furnishing, at all our public performances, the fullest and best orchestral force at their command. For their ability to do this, we are largely indebted to the enterprise and liberality of the Harvard Musical Association, in the education of the orchestra, and the encouragement they have given to orchestral performances of the highest order, by their admirable series of symphony concerts, established within the last two years.

And we see good reason to hope, in the thorough musical education which is now being given to the pupils of our public schools, and the further opportunities for musical study and practice, in the conservatories which have so lately sprung into being, that, for the future, our elements of growth, both choral and orchestral, will be abundantly increased.

A new edition of the Act of Incorporation and By-Laws of the society, containing the amendments recently adopted, together with such as may be added at the present or a future meeting, will soon be published, and placed in the hands of every member; and it is hoped that a more familiar acquaintance with the rules and regulations of our association, as thus set forth, will have its beneficial results.

It is a matter of congratulation for us, that, this year, the income from our special fund is left intact. An important consideration will be brought to your notice this evening, having reference to the prospective increase of the fund from the society's surplus receipts. I will not discuss this question in advance ; but will venture the hope that a way may be found to add to the investment, from time to time, from the moneys not needed for the current operations of the year, with the belief that our own example may, sooner or later, be followed by others outside our immediate circle.

In conclusion, I would call your attention to the fact that the coming year will furnish opportunity for the first in the regular series of triennial festivals, which, I believe, is to be the policy and purpose of the society to adopt — and of which the great festival of 1865, in commemoration of the birth of the second half-century of our existence, may, perhaps, with propriety, be considered the auspicious beginning. To that occasion we still look back with pride, as to a new starting-point in our own life, and an acknowledged era in the musical history of our country. I would advise that the main features of the programme should be early marked out and determined upon by the incoming Board, and the preliminary steps be taken in season to insure for it a success, artistically, at any rate, equal, if not superior to that of any former achievement. At the same time, I hope that the ordinary work of the year may not be materially interfered with, and that the regular concert season be not shorn of its goodly proportions, but that all things appertaining thereto be provided for, decently and in order, with unabated zeal and in its proper time.

With these words, gentlemen, again congratulating you upon the auspicious circumstances under which we have met together this evening, thanking you one and all for the part you have taken in the labors of the year now brought to a close, and with an earnest wish for your continued prosperity and success, I respectfully submit my report.

CPSIA information can be obtained
at www.ICGtesting.com
Printed in the USA
BVHW041027210219
540828BV00009B/185/P

9 780656 028603